MAZE
DECEPTION

Journey through Islam, Hinduisum, and Freemasonry, to finding the One True God

by Mick Oxley and Gaylene Odell

1st Edition - 2012

© 2012 Mick Oxley

In His Grip Ministries
206 Paradise Shores Road
Crescent City, FL, 32112 U.S.A.
Phone: (386) 698-2553
Email: ingrip@msn.com

Edited and Published by:
Life Application Ministries Publications (LAMP)
www.lamp@truthfrees.org

Printer: createspace.com

Clifford Dixon Arthur Oxley
(Mick)

Wing Commander
Royal Air Force A.F.C. (Ret.)

1923 - 2007

Index

Background 5
Dedication 6
Preface 7
Masonic Symbols 9
From Paganism to Christ 10
Searching for God in Islam 11
Searching for God in Hinduism 13
Searching for God in Freemasonry 15
Origin of Masonic Oaths 18
Yoked with Unbelievers 19
The Masonic god 21
The One True God 23
Deeds of Darkness 23
Set Free From Darkness 25
    PICTURES 28
Called to Ministry 30
The Mystic Shrine 31
Masonic Influence of England 33
Exposing the Occult 34
The Bondage of Masonry 37
Any God Will Do 38
Salvation By Works 40
The Secret Doctrine 42
Fraternal Orders 44
The Masonic Snare 45
Biography of the Author 49
Prayer of Release 52
Ministry Help and Contact Information 69
Recommended Reading 70
Works Cited 71

Background

This book was orginally produced many years ago by Mick, and since then, Gaylene - his daughter - continued to work on it and get it published. They have been told by many who have read the book, "This has to get in people's hands." So Gaylene has pursued this and now Mick's vision has come to pass.

Mick's testimony, until his passing, was always the same to "set the captives free". Now Gaylene, his daughter, has been passed the mantel to continue the work.

Though he mentions his search "through" other religions, it was the Freemasonry that he ended up serving the longest, which truly brought him into bondage.

It is vital to to recognize the power behind Masonry but to have compassion towards those who have been entraped as was Mick. But through prayer and the true Light of Jesus beaming into the dark areas of his life, he finally walked free of the bondage of Freemasonry.

Dedication

This book is dedicated to my mother who walked through this journey with my father leaving family and friends behind to travel to unknown lands as the role of a military wife.

To my sister Debbie who was part of this adventure and gracefully moved on from one station to the next.

To my wonderful husband and family who have supported, challenged , and encouraged me to continue *In His Grip Ministry.*

Most of all to I give Praise and thanks to Jesus, my Lord, who has carried me when I could not walk another step, showered me with the grace to go on despite how I felt and filled me with the desire and burden to see people freed from their bondage's.

Special Thanks

To Linda Lange (Life Application Ministries Publishing) who worked with me many hours to get this book published. She has helped make our desire for helping people know the truth about freemasonry, a reality.

Preface

I have been called to "sound the alarm" and in so doing, their blood will not be on my hands, for God will deal with these people who profess to walk in the light but are truly children of the dark and are blinded by rituals and traditions rather than God's Word!

I hope and pray that what I share in this book will change your family and friends thoughts about the truth of Freemasonry. The Mason's have a sign on their cars that say, "You have to be one to know one." Well, I was one and came out, realizing that I was following the wrong god. And if I can be freed, so can you. All it takes is getting down on your knees and in the name of Jesus, renounce your involvement in this demonic organization. I urge you to ask Jesus to become not just your Savior but Lord of your life. Don't play the Christian game of looking good in church, but live a life that is yielded to the Holy Spirit. Once you repent Jesus will forgive you and welcome you into His presence.

It is important that you notify your Lodge in writing that you have renounced Freemasonry. For it is contrary to the Christian beliefs, and by taking a stand in truth, do not be fearful of any retaliation or negative response because,

My Father, who has given them to me, is greater than all; no one can snatch them out of my Father's hand." John 10:29 (NIV).

Your letter to the lodge will be a witness which may in time cause others to come out. The Prayer of

Release is provided at the end of this book. It is to help you break the curses over you and your family's lives.

> *Do not be unequally yoked together with unbelievers. And what accord has Christ with Belial? Or what part has a believer with an unbeliever? And what agreement has the temple of God with idols? For you are the temple of the living God. As God has said: "I will dwell in them and walk among them. I will be their God, and they shall be My people." Therefore "Come out from among them And be separate, says the Lord. Do not touch what is unclean, and I will receive you. I will be a Father to you, and you shall be My sons and daughters, Says the LORD Almighty."*
>
> 2 Corinthians 6:14-18

In His Grip,
Mick Oxley

Masonic Symbols

SQUARE & COMPASS

"ALL SEEING EYE"

A CHURCH WINDOW

From Paganism to Christ

I spent more than 35 years with the Royal Air Force, traveling extensively, living in and visiting many countries throughout Europe, the Middle East, Africa, India, Malaysia, Singapore, Hong Kong and others.

In 1977, My wife and I came to America from Europe. We immigrated directly from NATO (North Atlantic Treaty Organization) in Norway, where I served with Allied Forces/Northern Europe at the Headquarters in Oslo.

I mention all my traveling because it's important that you understand how this related to the life I led years before I became Christian.

I had been brought up in the Anglican Faith as a nominal member of the Church of England, or Episcopalian as it is known here. I was confirmed at the age of twelve like every other member who called themselves "Christian." But, I really wasn't a Christian.

One doesn't become a Christian by joining the church. One becomes a Christian by receiving Jesus Christ as the Lord of their life. It is at this point that they are added to the body of Christ, the church. Joining a local congregation has nothing to do with whether or not your name is written in the Lamb's Book of Life.

It was during my operational air crew training in Egypt that I first came into contact with Islam, the Religion of the Muslim people. I was then a senior non-commissioned officer, a sergeant. We were living in tents in the Canal Zone alongside the Suez Canal in Egypt not far from the Great Bitter Lakes.

I remember as if it were yesterday, my servant, Abdul, coming to me and asking for a "chit"—a slip of paper upon which he wanted me to authorize his absence for the five daily times of prayer that his religion of Islam required. I could imagine what the British Trade Unions back in England would think of that!

I saw Abdul and hundreds of other Arab servants kneel down in the sand on little mats and pray to their god Allah five times a day! I was impressed. They were praying in the open, in full view of all of the Englishmen who, like me, were called "Christians."

Searching for God in Islam

At night time the Arab children would be allowed on base with their parents, our servants. The children, young boys from the ages of seven upwards would have Mullahs—teachers from the Arab Mosques from the towns and villages—teach them from the Quran, the Muslim Holy Book. Abdul acted as my interpreter telling me what the Mullahs were saying. I, along with my RAF friends, were shattered to hear the boys recite, word for word, chapter for chapter, from the Quran. I look back now as a Christian to the Vacation Bible School programs in Churches we have attended as a family where we have heard little Johnny, Susan and other children recite just one scripture from memory at the conclusion of the one week of Bible School. Yet, some of the Arab children could recite the entire Quran!

While we were in Cairo, many of my closest friends were recommended to take a course in Arabic. You may possibly appreciate the fact that Great Britain, under the League of Nations, had the mandate to rule Egypt, North Africa and Palestine—Israel as we know it today. We, as a country, were responsible for all of these territories. Since we had to insure that law and order was maintained, certain personnel were selected to learn the language of each of these territories. After all, it was necessary to be able to communicate with the residents and many of them did not speak English.

Those selected from the British Police and British services in Egypt and the other Arabic speaking countries under the mandate, attended Cairo University—the Institute for Islamic Studies in downtown Cairo. It was there that their Islamic studies began. Arabic was taught not from language training books, but from a pure Arabic source, the Quran itself. The instructors were the finest Arabic teachers in the world, the Mullahs or High Priests of Islam!

The selection of the Quran as the text book was not an accident. Not only were they taught Arabic, but by subtle indoctrination they became sympathetic toward the Muslim faith. The teaching of the Mullahs enabled them to view the Crusades from the Muslim perspective. The Mullahs were deeply grieved over the great loss of Muslim lives during the Holy wars. As a result, they were very bitter and they held a deep resentment toward, if not hatred for, Christians.

My friends were greatly moved emotionally when they heard the Muslim version of the massacre of the Muslims by our forefathers in the battles for Jerusalem and the Holy Land. They shared much of what they were learning with me and I obtained a good understanding of the Muslim faith, the religion of Islam.

Some of them began to see Islam as the true faith and a few actually embraced Islam, becoming Muslims. The Mullahs made much of the revenge they had enacted upon the Christians in the Arab conquest of North Africa. Many thousands of Christians were driven across North Africa to Morocco where they were slaughtered.

The thousands upon thousands of Muslim followers of Mohammed captured all of North Africa, Spain and as far north as France, only to be held back and defeated later on. I never forgot those teachings by the greatest authorities of Islam which were repeated to me by my closest friends.

I now understand that throughout my travels and experiences with Islam in the Middle East, North Africa and Egypt, I was searching for God. And I continued to search for God when I was transferred to India, home of the Hindu religion.

Searching for God in Hinduism

I first came into contact with Hinduism while stationed in New Delhi. We had a young Indian airman working with us in the Squadron at the RAF airport at Palam, New Delhi. These young men were very well educated Hindus, earmarked to take over from the British when we "quit India" after the Independence of Pakistan and the subsequent partitioning of the Muslims into what is now

Pakistan, Bangladesh and India.

The young students were exceptionally kind to single airmen who were away from their families and loved ones in England. We were frequently invited into their homes. It was a shock to all of the British to see how well-kept their houses were. They were immaculate.

After all, before meeting the Hindu airmen, all we had seen was abject poverty, and we employed the low caste of Indian people as our servants for five shillings, about seven dollars, a month! These poor souls thought of us as "White gods!" The respect the young men had for their families—bowing low to their fathers, saying prayers to their Hindu gods at meals—made a deep impression on me. In fact, I have never seen, even in America, so much prayer at meal times!

Many of my RAF compatriots and I became fascinated by the respect and prayers made to the Hindu gods. There were small idols of these gods in all of the Hindu households I visited. There was a special prayer closet where the families could go and meditate and ask the blessings of whatever god they turned to, to deal with a particular problem.

Those of us who expressed particular interest were taken by the families into their Hindu Temple. There are many sects or branches of Hinduism in India. Hindu Temple worship is by no means the same in all sects, but there are common characteristics which I found in all of the sects which I came

in contact with. I visited many Hindu temples of various sects in India.

I spent four years flying to and from every major city in India—Ceylon, Nepal, the cities in the North West Frontier and later Thailand and Burma—and one common activity which I saw in every Temple worship service as well as every Hindu wedding I attended, was the practice of circumambulation.

In circumambulation, they walked around the altar at least three times in a clockwise direction. This practice is of particular interest to our topic as will become clear as I tell you of my introduction into another religion, that of Freemasonry.

Searching for God in Freemasonry

I became a Freemason many years ago. We were living in Northern Ireland, and I was stationed at a Royal Air Force Radar Station on the coast south of Belfast. I had contemplated becoming a Freemason a few years before when we lived in Singapore on our first tour in Malaysia and Singapore. I was actually nominated for the Singapore Lodge, but my tour came to an end before I could go through any of the degrees.

I went through the first and second degrees, those of Entered Apprentice and the Fellowcraft degrees in Ireland under the Irish Constitution. Freemasonry is organized or administered under Constitutions in Europe rather than under jurisdictions as in the United States. This really amounts to nothing more than a difference in terminology.

I retained those recommendations and letters which I had received from members of Lodge Singapore, and I joined that lodge when we went back to Singapore a few years later.

The Royal Air Force reassigned me to Great Britain where I was able to complete the Master Mason degree in my home county of Yorkshire in the North of England. After completing the Master Mason degree, a man is as much a Mason as he will ever be. Going any higher, taking more degrees, does not enhance your status in Freemasonry. It may sound good to be a 32nd degree Mason, but the Lodges of Freemasonry World Wide work only in the first three degrees.

In English Freemasonry it takes many years to become a Master Mason. I was given special treatment because I was in the British services, and with the known nomadic life, I was rushed through, as most service members of English, Irish and Scottish Constitutions are. It's not that I was something special; I believe all members of Her Majesty's Forces who wished to become Freemasons received the same treatment.

The goals of Masons in Europe are quite different than those in America. Once you are a Master Mason in Britain, you work through the Chairs to become the Worshipful Master of your home Lodge. That is the greatest goal of an English Master Mason and it usually took many years to achieve. The Worshipful Masters I encountered seemed to be "old men," at least to me!

Lodges here in America tend to be much larger than their European counterparts, sometimes with several hundred members. The average American Freemason has less of a chance than his English counterpart to serve for a year as the Master of his Lodge. This may partially explain the necessity for the many separate degrees in the Scottish Rite and the great number of additional American Masonic bodies such as the Grotto and the Mystic Shrine.

I was not a Christian when I joined Freemasonry, although I knew much of the teachings of Christianity due to having attended the Church of England. I also was never a confirmed Muslim or Hindu, although I had learned much of those religious beliefs as well.

As I said, I first joined Freemasonry under the Irish Constitution in Ireland. I went on to take the degree of Master Mason under the English Constitution in England. Later, after being transferred to Africa, I entered a Lodge which was operated under the Constitution of Scotland. The rituals of all of these lodges were in all essential details, identical.

I needed only the first degree to convince me that what I was into was evil. Within the first ten minutes into the Entered Apprentice Degree, I took evil oaths, really putting a curse upon myself in the swearing of this oath: "I do most solemnly and sincerely promise and swear, binding myself under no less a penalty than to have my throat cut across, my tongue torn out by the roots, so help me God."

This oath is direct disobedience to one of the commands of Jesus. In Matthew 5, verses 34 through 37 Jesus said:

> *"But I say to you, make no oath at all, either by heaven, for it is the throne of God, or by the earth, for it is the footstool of His feet, or by Jerusalem, for it is THE CITY OF THE GREAT KING. Nor shall you make an oath by your head, for you cannot make one hair white or*

black. But let your statement be, 'Yes, yes' or 'No, no'; and anything beyond these is of evil."

Origin of Masonic Oaths

On my first night in the lodge, I was required to disobey God and break one of His commands. I had to break these commandments by taking another hideous oath every time I took another degree. More than this, I recognized these evil oaths! They were identical to Hindu Temple worship!

I had witnessed Hindu Temple worship during my nearly four years serving in India and had studied the Hindu faith. I marveled at the intertwining of the two religions—Hinduism and Freemasonry. And as I went up through the higher degrees, I found more of the same evil curses and oaths from Hinduism.

Another familiar aspect of the Masonic ritual in the Entered Apprentice, the Fellowcraft and the Master Mason degree is the rite of circumambulation.

When a candidate goes through a degree, he and the officers of the lodge walk around the lodge three times in a clockwise direction. I knew it came directly from the Hindu Temple worship. There could be no doubt since I was familiar with the Hindu worship ceremonies!

Remember, I laid no claim to being a Christian at that time. But I had been brought up in the Anglican Faith as a nominal member of the Church of England, so I knew enough to know that what I was saying and doing was against Jesus Christ and the Bible.

While we were living in England, I became a masonic zealot attending and visiting as many English Lodges in England as I could, really as my income would allow. I was spending more of my service pay on Freemasonry and the Masonic Charities than on my family. Freemasonry is expensive, perhaps more so in England with the Masonic dinners—always in evening dress, Tuxedos as it is called over here. I attended meetings many times in the Grand Lodge of England on Great Queen Street.

The Grand Lodge of England is the Mother Lodge of the World. Freemasonry started in England in the early 18th century and then spread to the rest of the world. Great Britain was a great world power at the time and she had colonies in all parts of the world.

Yoked with Unbelievers

The Royal Air Force transferred me back to Singapore. After settling in, I became a member of what can be called one of the most prestigious Masonic Lodges in the world, namely, "Lodge Singapore." As its name suggests, it is located in the city of Singapore, on the island of Singapore.

It was in this Lodge that I first met members who were Muslims, Hindus, Buddhists, Chinese Taoists, Shintoists, Jains, Sikhs, Jews—and so called Christians—whose religions I was familiar with from my travels in the Middle East, Europe, Africa and India.

We had on display more than five Volume of the Sacred Law. The Bible is not called a Bible in Freemasonry, it is just one of the Holy books of a particular religion—the Quran for the Muslim brethren, the Bhagavad Gita for the Hindu and so on. When taking a degree, each candidate swears the oath on the Holy Book of his particular religion. These men of these different religions were all full members of the Lodge, and some of them held officer positions within the Lodge. As I recall, during part of my time in the Lodge, the Worshipful Master was a Muslim and the Senior Warden, a Hindu.

In America the Lodges are segregated with African Americans having their own lodge called "Prince Hall" because Albert Pike, a renown leading authority on American Freemasonry, was a racist and one of the founding members of the Ku Klux Klan (KKK).

After serving in Singapore for nearly three years, I was posted back to England. But after a brief time there, I was on the move again, this time to Zambia in Africa where I joined a lodge operating under the Scottish Constitution. The lodge was located in Lusaka, the capital city of Zambia. There were Hindus, Muslims and several other pagan religions represented in the Scottish Lodge in Zambia. However, after being a member in Lodge Singapore, I hardly noticed.

The Masonic god

After being posted back again to England, I decided to take the Royal Arch Degree. It was this degree which really made me see the extent of the evil of Freemasonry.

The Royal Arch degree is pretty much the same in America as in Europe. Royal Arch Masons gather around what is called an altar or Ark, and call out using the secret name of God which is supposedly known only by Royal Arch Masons. They call upon the pagan god of Freemasonry, "JAH BUL ON." Each of the three men forming the "Holy Royal Arch" speaks a syllable in rapid succession.

The word JAH BUL ON is supposed to have been rediscovered in some long forgotten vault. It is the secret name of the Masonic god, whom Masons refer to as "The Great Architect of the Universe." This "lost name of God" is found only in the Royal Arch degree.

After the ritual I asked my fellow Royal Arch Masons who had been in the order for several years about the true meaning behind the word JAH-BUL-ON. I was told that Jah is supposed by some to be short for Yahweh, the God of the Christian and Jew, BUL is a rendering of the name BAAL or BEL, the ancient name of the Canaanite god. ON or LUN was supposed to be the Chaldean name of God.

The name Baal seemed vaguely familiar to me. After being given these explanations, I went home and began searching the scriptures. I found Baal in 1st Kings, chapter 18. There, Elijah challenged Ahab and the other prophets of Baal at Mt. Carmel. Elijah suggested they build an altar to Baal. He told them to put an ox on their altar and to put wood around it but not to set it on fire. Then Elijah said, "You call on the name of your god, and I will call on the name of the LORD, and the God who answers by fire, He is God." All of the people answered and said, "That is a good idea."

The prophets of Baal called on Baal from morning until evening without any answer. Elijah then rebuilt the altar of the Lord which had been torn down and cut a bull into pieces. He placed the bull on top of the wood on the altar and had water poured over the altar three times. The water overflowed and filled a trench which had been dug around the altar. Elijah then called upon the Lord one time. Fire came down from heaven and consumed the altar, the sacrifice and even the water in the trench. The prophets of Baal fell upon their faces and yelled, "The Lord, he is God!" Then Elijah the prophet of the Lord God commanded that all of the prophets of Baal be rounded up. Elijah had them all killed.

I realized that this name of the Masonic Deity, JAH-BUL-ON is a three headed pagan god, so remote from the Christian faith and so blasphemous as to damn the eternal soul of anyone who would dare to pronounce its name in worship! It is spiritual insanity for a Christian to stand at this altar with others, some vicars, clergymen, lawyers, businessmen of all religions and creeds—Hindus, Muslims, Jews, Buddhists, and men of other faiths—and cry out this unholy name in ritual and worship.

Here then is revealed the true identity of the Masonic god, the Great Architect of the Universe! Freemasonry amounts to nothing less than BAAL worship.

The ritual and a full explanation of what I have just shared can be found in Duncan's Masonic Ritual and Monitor. Duncan closely agrees with the rituals which I practiced as an Irish, English and then Scottish Freemason.

From its very beginnings in England, then in Europe and the rest of the world, Freemasonry has lied to and deceived its members by this subtle trickery. Even those who are taught the "Ineffable Name" of the pagan Masonic god, JAH-BUL-ON, do not understand or appreciate the truth behind this name, because of the deliberate deception used. The truth is intentionally hidden throughout the Masonic degrees, in the ritual itself, hidden by the leaders, and the members are taught—as I was—that the brethren in Masonic leadership would never lie to a Brother Mason! That is the biggest lie in Freemasonry!

The One True God

In 1969 I found the "One True God" I had been seeking. My oldest daughter went to a Christian concert and accepted Jesus Christ as her personal Lord and Savior. I saw a visible change in her life and wanted what she had, so I too became a Christian. My wife and my other daughter also accepted Jesus and we were all joined to the local church of which my youngest daughter still attends.

Deeds of Darkness

Due to my training in the occult teachings of Hinduism, I could not help but recognize in the words and symbols used in Masonic ritual the influence and direction of the occult—the very things I had seen in Eastern Mysticism in India years before.

As a Christian, I now know that it's author is Satan himself! This Masonic Ritual was from the Underworld, the darkness that the Lord Jesus Christ exhorts us in His Word to separate ourselves from. The very fact that all Masonic rituals are practiced in secret shows a sharp contrast to the nature of our Lord, Jesus Christ. In John 18:20 Jesus said, *"I have spoken openly to the world; I always taught in synagogues, and in the temple, where all the Jews come together; and I spoke nothing in secret."*

Paul wrote to the Ephesians, exhorting them in chapter 5, verse 11: *"Do not participate in the unfruitful deeds of darkness, but instead even expose them."*

However, for me, following my installation into Royal Arch Freemasonry, it was second Corinthians that spoke directly to my heart, my spirit: *"Therefore, come out from their midst and be separate,"* says the Lord. *"And do not touch what is unclean; And I will welcome you."*

He was saying to me—"come out of Masonry and be separate. Touch not the unclean thing," meaning the Masonic square and compass, the altar of Freemasonry, the Masonic Bible, the jewels, sash, aprons and all the host of trappings that I had taken on with my degrees as a zealous Freemason. "Come out and be separate and I will receive you."

Set Free From Darkness

One day in Holland where I was living, I came to do just that. I left behind the Quran and its teachings of Mohammed and Islam, and the Bhagavad Gita of Hinduism. Now I had attempted to make my standard the Holy Bible and Jesus Christ. I knew there was no other way!

But there was still no fullness in my life. The words of Jesus found in Matthew 7:21 23 spoke to me:

"Not everyone who says to Me, 'Lord, Lord,' will enter the kingdom of heaven; but he who does the will of My Father who is in heaven. Many will say to Me on that day, 'Lord, Lord, did we not prophesy in Your name, and in Your name cast out demons, and in Your name perform many miracles?' And then I will declare to them, 'I never knew you; DEPART FROM ME, YOU WHO PRACTICE LAWLESSNESS.'"

The words spoke directly to me: "You call me Jesus, your Savior, your Lord—yet you practice things I have not taught you. Depart from me, I never knew you; you are a worker of evil."

I yearned for a one on one walk with Jesus. I asked advice of my fellow officers and friends in the American Church on the base in Holland where we lived. They had no good answer because they didn't understand Freemasonry. My American friends told me that I was just a "back slider." They didn't recognize that I was being led by the Holy Spirit to accept Jesus as the Lord of my life. I was a member of the church, but I had not yet been filled with the Holy Spirit.

I finally got down on my knees, as I should have done long ago, and asked Jesus what was wrong! One word came back to me as though shouted from heaven, "Freemasonry!" I knew in a flash that I was in trouble with the real God. As if I need confirmation, a letter came that very morning from our youngest daughter, Debbie, in London. In the letter she said, "You have to get out of Freemasonry, Dad! You know it is evil, it is Satanic, and you will never walk with God until you do".

That day my wife, Betty, helped me burn all my Masonic Regalia—my aprons of all the degrees I had been through, my gloves, gauntlets, sashes, charity jewels—presented to me because of my support of the Royal Masonic Hospital, the Royal Masonic Schools for both boys and girls, all my Masonic books, certificates, and everything connected with Freemasonry.

Betty prayed with me while I repented of ever being a Mason. I confessed my sin of evil. I broke the Satanic curses upon me from Freemasonry, from Islam and Hinduism. But I knew that the bondage of Freemasonry was much stronger than any other of the occult religions!

After all my wanderings and searching, I was able to finally separate myself from the Spirit of Darkness and repent, and confess and ask God's forgiveness of all of the evil in which I had been a participant. The Lord Jesus Christ heard my cry, and for the first time in my life, I felt the weight of all that evil lift off me. As Jesus said in John Chapter 8, *"If therefore the Son shall make you free, you shall be free indeed."*

I then came into the Spirit filled Life of Jesus Christ. My life changed from that moment. The scriptures in the Bible became fully alive to me. My love for His Word and His people eventually led me into the Ministry He has given me.

Mick and Betty Oxley

Mick's Air Crew

Masons - 32 degree

Mick entering Mosque (far right)

Servants in India

Called to the Ministry

I came out of the Royal Air Force a few years later, at the peak of my career. I was a Senior Officer with the rank of Wing Commander. That would be equivalent to the rank of Commander in the American Navy.

I left the Royal Air Force for one reason: the Lord called me to get out and come and serve The King for the rest of my life—for most of my life, since boyhood I had been serving the Queen.

We left everything, including a home in England and our friends in Europe. We made a complete break with Great Britain, immigrated to the United States and became American citizens in the minimum time allowed, five years. It is a decision we have never regretted.

The Lord called me to the Ministry. He gave me seven years to be equipped to minister, then I was ordained, to go out "into all the World and proclaim the Gospel of Jesus Christ." This is what this message is all about, to proclaim the truth, to proclaim Jesus.

The Lord confirmed the Ministry through a prophecy which was given when I came to this country. I really do not care if you believe in prophecy, but I am telling you He gave it to me, to be followed by the formation of "In His Grip Ministries."

I repeat this prophecy, this direction, that the Lord gave me:

> "Teach the Truth about the religion of Islam, and those occultic religions covered by the name of Eastern Mysticism and to expose the Satanic influence in the background of Freemasonry. I have allowed you to go into these religions so that by the Truth of My Word and your experiences you will be fully equipped to carry My message to the World."

This has been the burning desire of my heart ever since.

The Mystic Shrine

It was after we moved to America that I first encountered the Mystic Shrine, or to give this American degree its full name, "The Ancient Arabic Order Nobles of the Mystic Shrine." This is a purely American degree which indeed would not be tolerated by British Freemasons. This is an adolescent degree of childish behavior and wild parties including blasphemies which serves as its ritual. The solemn obligation is utter blasphemy in which the candidate takes the oath of a Muslim and declares Allah, the god of Arab, Muslim and Mohammed to be "the God of our fathers." It is obvious that Allah is not the God of the Bible because Allah does not have a son. Allah is actually a demon spirit as are all gods worshiped in all other pagan religions.

Other elements of the Shriner's ritual have been recognized for what they are by Anton LaVey, in his book, The Satanic Rituals. LaVey describes himself in the book as one of the Devil's most devoted disciples.

He also wrote the Satanic Bible and was founder of the California based Church of Satan.

In "The Satanic Rituals," LaVey describes one of the rites of Lucifer, called L'Air Epais. In English, it is translated as The Ceremony of the Stifling Air. LaVey writes:

"A striking American parallel to this rite is enacted within the mosques of the Ancient Arabic Order of the Nobles of the Mystic Shrine, an order reserved for thirty-second degree Masons. The Nobles have gracefully removed themselves from any implication of heresy by referring to the place beyond the Devil's Pass as the domain where they might worship at the shrine of Islam.'"

It really makes little difference whether one worships Allah or the Devil. Both are demonic. While I watched the Shriner's parade for the first time in America, I saw the Fez. I was horrified. I immediately remembered the teachings about the Fez given by the Mullahs which my friends had repeated to me in Egypt. The Mullahs had bragged of the Muslim hoards which had driven thousands of Christians across the northern part of Africa to the city of Fez, Morocco.

They bragged that at Fez, the Muslims took revenge for their losses during the Crusades by executing fifty thousand Christian men, women and children. The Mullahs said that even unborn babies were murdered, being removed from the wombs of their mothers and having their heads, arms and legs hacked off with the scimitar, a large sword with a curved blade. They boasted that the blood of the slaughtered Christians was running deep in the streets of Fez and the Muslim executioners dipped their white hats into the Christian's blood and proudly placed the now blood-red hats on their heads as symbols of their triumph. These red hats were known as *Fezes* from that time forward.

I was deeply grieved to see the Shriners proudly wearing this red Fez. They also were displaying the Muslim emblem of the crescent moon and star along with the emblem of the scimitar which was used to put to death these thousands of Christian men, women and children in Fez, Morocco—the same scimitar that the Mullahs also said would ultimately be used against all infidels throughout the world who do not bow down and worship Allah. God must look upon the Shriners with utter disgust and loathing as they parade around like stupid school children.

Masonic Influence of England

I know that in English Freemasonry, the blood oaths in the first three degrees and in the Royal Arch degree have now been removed. Do not be fooled! I renounced English Masonry because I knew it was evil. I knew it had occultic overtones. Because of my experience in Eastern Mysticism, I was not just uncomfortable being a Mason, my spirit became absolutely distressed.

Since renouncing Freemasonry, I have become aware of the hidden spiritual forces of darkness and the subversive political influence of Masonry. I have reviewed the different church pronouncements concerning Freemasonry. Many of those studies in England and in Western Europe have been performed independently from one another.

This adds credibility to the unanimous conclusion that Freemasonry is in reality an instrument of deception by our adversary, Satan. It is without question one of his most successful and formidable accomplishments.

It became quite apparent to me how Masonry has influenced Great Britain, in particular through the agency of the police. Scotland Yard was unduly influenced by Freemasons who held high positions. The Metropolitan Police and the Justice System have also been taken captive by the spirit of Freemasonry. Justice is not applied equally to Masons and non Masons. This has been reported in several books, including The Brotherhood, by Stephen Knight and Inside the Brotherhood, by Martin Short. Both of these books are sold in England.

The influence of Freemasonry within the Royal Family should leave little doubt as to why the "Royals are in a mess." Her Majesty, the Queen, is the patron of Freemasonry. The Duke of Kent is the Grand Master of the Mother Lodge of the world, the Grand Lodge of England. His brother is also a Mason. The Queen's husband, Prince Philip, is a Freemason. The Royal princes and Kings of England have been Freemasons since the foundation of the Grand Lodge of England, bringing the curse of Freemasonry upon the royal household and Great Britain as a nation.

Exposing the Occult

We live in Crescent City, in Central Florida. Our ministry is small by most evangelical standards, but there are few ministries like it. In fact, there are only about seven or eight ministries in the world working full time to expose the evils of Freemasonry. Also, there are few Christian missionaries working with Muslims and Hindus. I am blessed to be working to expose Islam, the Occult nature of Hinduism and Eastern Mysticism and their relationship to Freemasonry.

Frankly, it is not easy, but then the Lord says it never will be! We are on duty for the Lord 24 hours per day. We send out material all over the United States and the rest of the World, trying to help people who have become entangled in false religions. We have a special burden for those who have become ensnared in the Masonic system. So many have come into bondage due to the evil of Freemasonry.

We have ministered to hundreds of people who have come under bondage and curses from the "Sins of their Fathers" (and Mothers.) The Bible is plain on these curses, and you will find the references to what I am speaking about in the following scriptures.

Exodus 20:3-6

> *³Thou shalt have no other gods before me. ⁴Thou shalt not make unto thee any graven image, or any likeness of any thing that is in heaven above, or that is in the earth beneath, or that is in the water under the earth. ⁵Thou shalt not bow down thyself to them, nor serve them: for I the Lord thy God am a jealous God, visiting the iniquity of the fathers upon the children unto the third and fourth generation of them that hate me; ⁶And shewing mercy unto thousands of them that love me, and keep my commandments.*

Exodus 34:7

Keeping mercy for thousands, forgiving iniquity and transgression and sin, and that will by no means clear the guilty; visiting the iniquity of the fathers upon the children, and upon the children's children, unto the third and to the fourth generation.

Deuteronomy 5:9-10

[9]Thou shalt not bow down thyself unto them, nor serve them: for I the Lord thy God am a jealous God, visiting the iniquity of the fathers upon the children unto the third and fourth generation of them that hate me, [10]And shewing mercy unto thousands of them that love me and keep my commandments.

Numbers 14:8

If the Lord delight in us, then he will bring us into this land, and give it us; a land which floweth with milk and honey.

Deuteronomy 28:15

But it shall come to pass, if thou wilt not hearken unto the voice of the Lord thy God, to observe to do all his commandments and his statutes which I command thee this day; that all these curses shall come upon thee, and overtake thee:

From verses 16-66 names all the dis-eases and curses upon a person who practices false religions. And these are the same curses and dis-eases that fall onto our family. What God is saying in these passages, and many other scriptures, is that curses for the sins of your forefathers, at least back to the third and forth generation, will be passed down to your generation. Sins that are an abomination to God are things like witchcraft, or the sin of rebellion, bowing down to idols, making oaths, etc. Involvement in Freemasonry, which participates in these sins, is a prime example of a religious order that can affect not only the Mason, but can affect his children, his grandchildren and even their children.

The Bondage of Masonry

Someone asked me, "Mick, with all your experience in the Occult of Hinduism, Islam and Freemasonry, with the years you've now spent in the ministry, what do find you is the strongest bondage placed over a person?"

Without the slightest hesitation, or even having to think, I replied, "Freemasonry. I have no doubt whatsoever, that the strongest bondage anyone can experience is the curse of Freemasonry!" Simply put, it means that if your parents or ancestors were involved in sins which are an abomination to Our Lord God, the curse will be passed down to you.

We have found in this ministry, and this has been confirmed by countless other ministries, that the bondage, the curse of Freemasonry will be upon your life forever if you or your ancestors have indulged in the occult of Freemasonry.

You can be set free, as I was those years ago, by renouncing the involvement of your family, or yourself, asking the Lord's forgiveness, repenting of the involvement, and asking the Lord to set you free. It is just that simple. But believe me, friends, it is vital for your life that you obey the Word of Almighty God. We have seen hundreds of people set free from this particular curse of Freemasonry and others. Praise God—their lives have been changed!

Deuteronomy 28:1-2 says:

> *¹And it shall come to pass, if thou shalt hearken diligently unto the voice of the Lord thy God, to observe and to do all his commandments which I command thee this day, that the Lord thy God will set thee on high above all nations of the earth: ²And all these blessings shall come on thee, and overtake thee, if thou shalt hearken unto the voice of the Lord thy God.*

So, when we decide to make Jesus Christ our Lord, accept what He did on the cross to pay for our sins, when we submit to the truth found in the Word of God, blessings will follow, curses will be broken, bondages and chains will fall off, not only from us, but our children and children's children as well.

It is not always an easy life, but then Jesus never said it would be! But, oh the Glory of bringing people to Him, helping to get people freed from the bondage of sin and death that they have picked up in their life, by their own doing or from their generations.

Any God Will Do

I have said, on the record, many times before, and I will say it again: Christianity and Freemasonry are incompatible. I made no pretence of being a Christian when I went into Freemasonry, yet I knew that what I was doing and saying was against the Word of God. I knew that Freemasonry was incompatible with Christianity. I simply am unable to understand how any man who is a Christian could enter the Lodge, take those blood oaths, and then take part in worship of the Masonic god known as the Great Architect of the Universe. I suppose it depends on what sort of a Christian you are!

Even today many people, even some in the church, believe that the Masonic Lodge is just a social organization whose members are Christians. They could never be more wrong! The group of people in "Lodge Singapore" certainly did not profess to be Christians.

Freemasonry does not require faith in Jesus Christ, but only belief in a Supreme Being. Any god will do. Thus a man can worship his Supreme Being as Buddha, Krishna, Baal, Osiris or Jesus—it makes no difference in Masonry. Masonry teaches that there is only one God and men of all the different religions worship that one God using a variety of different names.

Of course, Christians know that such a teaching is Biblical nonsense. Paul's first letter to the Church at Corinth wrote that, "The sacrifices of pagans are offered to demons, not to God." When a Buddhist worships his demon god in the Lodge, he refers to him as the Great Architect of the Universe. Similarly, the Hindu, the Muslim, the Sikh, the Taoist, all refer to the Great Architect of the Universe, finding this name a suitable representation of their demon gods.

As I mentioned, in the Royal Arch Degree, the god of Freemasonry—the Great Architect of the

Universe—is identified as Jah Bul ON. But Yahweh, the God of Abraham, Isaac and Jacob, simply cannot be worshiped in the same service with Baal and other false gods! All of the men who participate in the pagan rituals in the lodge, worshiping the Great Architect of the Universe, are simply worshiping a demon.

Since Freemasonry includes men of many pagan demonic religions who worship false gods, it should be pretty clear to you by now that the Masonic Lodge is NOT a Christian organization!

Salvation By Works

We come now to this question: What, then, does Freemasonry teach about the vital doctrine of salvation? In the Entered Apprentice degree, the ritual contains the following words: "The covering of a Lodge is a clouded canopy, or star-decked heaven, where all good Masons hope at last to arrive..." The ritual specifically states that as a good Mason I should hope to go to heaven!

In the third, or Master Mason degree, the ritual states: "As Fellow Crafts, we should apply our knowledge to the discharge of our respective duties to God, our neighbors and ourselves, so that in age, as Master Masons, we may enjoy the happy reflections consequent on a well spent life, and die in the hope of a glorious immortality!"

I was told through the ritual that as a Master Mason I should die in the hope of a glorious immortality. In the third degree ritual, I heard the Worshipful Master's prayer: "Yet, O Lord, have compassion on the children of thy creation, administer them comfort in time of trouble, and save them with everlasting salvation. Amen!"

Masonry teaches that Master Masons, as a group, may die in the hope of a glorious immortality, that Masons represent those raised from the grave of iniquity, and that they may have redemption from the death of sin. Freemasonry is teaching that Master Masons may have salvation—whether, Christian, Muslim, Jew, Hindu—or whatever!

This is done not just in England, Scotland, Ireland and Singapore but here in the United States as well. I have seen Monitors for about half of the Grand Lodges in the United States and they all contain the same teaching.

However, the Holy Bible is quite clear: Jesus Christ is the only way to salvation. Peter speaking of Jesus, said in Acts 4:12: *"There is salvation in no one else; for there is no other name under heaven that has been given among men, by which we must be saved."*

And in John 14:6, Jesus said: *"I am the Way, the Truth, and the Life: no one comes to the Father, but through Me."*

I am sure you are aware that in the first century Church some thought that they could be Christians and still participate in pagan (non-Christian) religions. Paul spoke very clearly to this issue in his letter to the Corinthian Church:

1 Corinthians 10:20-21

> [21]*But I say, that the things which the Gentiles sacrifice, they sacrifice to devils, and not to God:*

and I would not that ye should have fellowship with devils. ²¹Ye cannot drink the cup of the Lord, and the cup of devils: ye cannot be partakers of the Lord's table, and of the table of devils. (KJV)

Now the question arises as to whether there are Christians in the Masonic Lodge. My reply is this: The Masonic Lodge continues to ensnare men, and some who join are Christians. Some of them recognize the pagan nature of Masonry the first night in the Lodge and simply never go back. Sometimes a Christian is compelled by the Holy Spirit to get out of the Lodge without knowing at the time all of the reasons why he had to end his involvement with Freemasonry. Some reason that if their Pastor, an Elder or a Deacon from their congregation is also involved in Masonry, there can't be anything wrong with it. But, sooner or later they realize that Freemasonry offers a plan of salvation without Jesus. The teachings about salvation are not hidden from them. They have taken part in rituals which teach salvation and usually they have watched and listened as others have gone through the ritual.

I maintain that no true Christian will or can remain in an organization which teaches salvation without Jesus Christ, whether the organization claims to be Christian or not.

The Secret Doctrine

In my travels as a zealous Freemason, I was told there was much more to Freemasonry than what I would see and take part in through ritual. I was told that to go deeper into Freemasonry, I would have to investigate the teachings contained in Masonic books. Some spoke of a Secret Doctrine which was not taught in the ritual. I know from my years of visiting Lodges, as a Freemason, world wide, that each Lodge has a library containing books that may be borrowed by the aspiring Mason.

Additionally, these books are made available by suppliers to the craft. There are two stores across the street from the Grand Lodge of England where I attended which sell these books. It costs a considerable sum of money to run a shop like this. Rent, utilities, salaries and the like have to be offset by the sales of books and other merchandise. If Masons were not buying these books and other items the regalia shops would not have remained in the business for over 200 years. If Masonic books did not continue to sell, the publishers which print them could not remain in business. I have examined the catalogs from Masonic suppliers in the United States and can testify that the most of the books which are in use in England are also available in the United States through American Masonic suppliers such as Macoy Publishing and Masonic Supply Company.

The Secret Doctrine of the Masonic Lodge is the ultimate proof that Freemasonry is totally incompatible with Christianity. The Secret doctrine teaches that Jesus Christ is not the only begotten Son of God, but that each Mason may become a Christ through a process known as Masonic Initiation. The Secret Doctrine teaches that since he may become a Christ, each Mason is his own Savior—if he does not save himself, he will not be saved. The process of initiation is not a ceremony, but a process wherein the Mason goes into a trance and attains conscious union with the god of the Lodge. The Secret Doctrine draws heavily from the occult teachings of Hinduism and Eastern Mysticism

which I know only too well. I know that few Masons—
and even fewer non Masons—have an accurate
conception of the true nature of Freemasonry.

I have tried to show you the pagan nature of
Freemasonry. I have explained that Freemasonry has
its own plan of salvation. In the Secret Doctrine, it
becomes clear that we are indeed delving deep into
the Occult of Freemasonry.

The Secret Doctrine is well documented in the
literature of Freemasonry. If you doubt this, you need
to check only one book: *The Builders*, by Joseph Fort
Newton. It is available from Macoy in this country
and is found in the libraries of most lodges world
wide. Chapter four is entitled *The Secret Doctrine*. *The
Builders* does not explain well the Secret Doctrine,
but the author recommends many books which do.
Newton lifts up Arthur Edward Waite as the greatest
student of the Secret Doctrine. Waite's writings are
full of mysticism and occultism.

Fraternal Orders

Fraternal orders are organizations whose
members are usually bound by an oath and who
make extensive use of secret ritual in the conduct
of their meetings. Most fraternal orders are limited
to members of one sex, although some include both
men and women. The best-known orders are the
Freemasons (see Freemasonry) and the Odd Fellows,
both of which originated in 18th-century England
(although enthusiasts have placed the origin of
the Freemasons at the time of the construction of
Solomon's Temple). Most American fraternal orders
were established in the 19th cent. Many were formed
for a special purpose or for the benefit of particular

groups; e.g., the Patrons of Husbandry, or the Grange (see Granger movement), was founded to improve the lot of the farmer and was for a time an important political force. To a large degree, though, these organizations expressed a desire to establish principally male rituals. The Knights of Columbus was formed (1882) to provide a fraternal order for Roman Catholics free of the oath-taking requirement to which they were opposed. Other orders, founded when commercial insurance companies did not extend coverage to workers, provided sickness and death benefits to members. That function of fraternal orders declined as insurance companies expanded their coverage, and today most fraternal orders serve mainly as charitable institutions and social centers. Other well-known fraternal orders and their years of founding in the United States are the Order of Hibernians (1836), Knights of Pythias (1864), Fraternal order of Eagles and Elks Benevolent and Protective Order (1868).

See M. C. Carnes, Meanings for Manhood (1990)

The Masonic Snare

I have nothing but compassion for those who have been ensnared in Freemasonry. I know only too well the bondage they are under. They are deceived—intentionally—as I was. I was eventually able to see through it because of my background in other occult religions.

The Lord allowed me to go into Freemasonry just as he allowed me to go into Islam and Eastern Mysticism, right into the bottom of the pit of Hell. Then finally, He brought me out—when I had screamed and yelled enough and at last was able through the prayers of my wife and family to ask His forgiveness, repent of my sins, and thus be SET FREE in Jesus Christ.

I said at the beginning that the greatest bondage in the world today is the occult organization of Freemasonry. It's true, hidden purpose is to remove God from His throne in the lives of the men whom it has ensnared. It is Anti-Christian and it has, by occultic means, greater control over human beings than any other demonic organization.

Why then do Christians continue their relationship with Freemasonry, in spite of the fact that they claim to know what Christianity is, and also what Freemasonry is? If they truly do understand the real purposes of Freemasonry, they are without excuse. They are living a deliberate lie and are being intentionally disloyal to the Lord Jesus Christ, who died for their sins!

Most Freemasons who are professing Christians are apostate from the true faith. Some of the Pastors and other church leaders who are in Masonry belong in this classification. They have relegated truths such as the Blood Atonement and the Deity of Christ to the place of non essentials. I have been called to sound the alarm. In so doing, their blood will not be on my hands—God will deal with these people.

I hope and pray that, through what I have shared with you, you will be able to understand that Freemasonry is specifically Anti-Christian. It cannot and will not have a good effect in your life, the lives of your family members or the church as a whole.

If you are now a Freemason, I urge you to get down on your knees and call out to the God of Abraham, Isaac and Jacob, the God of the Bible, in the name of Jesus and renounce your involvement in this evil organization. I urge you to ask Jesus to become your Savior and the Lord and Master of your life. Ask God to set you free and fill you with the Holy Spirit.

If you do, I can assure you that your life will take a turn for the better. You will come to know Jesus as you have never known Him before. Jesus is willing to forgive you. He wants to forgive you, but his forgiveness is conditional on your repentance. Don't wait any longer. You have seen enough in the ritual to know that what I have told you is true.

It is important that you notify your lodge in writing that you are renouncing Freemasonry. You can simply say that you have found it to be incompatible with Christianity and therefore you can't have any more to do with it. It would be good to have a fellow Christian witness the letter. Your letter to the lodge will be a witness which may in time cause others to come out. Even if no one else renounces because of your letter, you will have set them on notice and you won't have to stand before God with their blood on you hands.

As the Apostle Paul said, "Come out from among them and be ye separate, says the Lord!"

It is important to state here that if your family either alive or deceased was ever involved in Freemasonry, then there is a generational curse upon your family line. It will effect you even though you yourself have never been involved. You need to renounce it and break the curse over your family even future generations. The "Prayer of Release" that will help you break all the curses that are spoken by your family members that to this day are manifesting in your family line.

Nehemiah 9:2

And the seed of Israel separated themselves from all strangers, and stood and confessed their sins, and the iniquities of their fathers.

Biography of the Author (Mick)

Mick Oxley was born into an upper middle class family in Yorkshire England. He was expected to attend the local Church of England every Sunday and he became a choirboy. Nothing sparked his interest in God and outwardly appeared to be a "Christian" young man. However he never heard God mentioned in his home. Later at the age of 18 he joined the Royal Air Force and served 35 years for Queen and country.

During his service he traveled throughout the world and for many years served as personal air crew to Prime Ministers, and high dignitaries worldwide. While on assignment for Her Majesty in the Middle East, Mick became involved in Islam. He lived with Muslims for over fifteen years of his life. His crew flew Winston Churchill, Lord Mountbatten and his wife plus other well known personalities. He became an officer and eventually retired at the rank of Wing Commander.

Meanwhile stationed in India he became interested in Hinduism and Eastern Mysticism. He entered these religions searching for the true Light of truth and sat under Mahatma Gandi's teaching.

After returning to another assignment in England he married his childhood sweetheart Betty. In 1952 he received the Air Force Cross for his service to His Majesty from Queen Elizabeth 11.

Along with his wife and his two children were assigned to Singapore, Malaya, and various posting in the United Kingdom and served unaccompanied in South Africa.

After returning to England to another assignment, Mick completed his Master Mason degree in Freemasonry in the English Constitution, which is the world's oldest. Then during his tour of duty in Zambia, Central Africa, he came under the Scottish Constitution of Freemasonry.

Finally, in 1967, Mick found the truth he had been searching for all these years. Gaylene his eldest daughter had given her life to Jesus in a youth rally at a local church. Mick saw this change in her and visited a local church where he too accepted Jesus into his life. This was the end of his search and the beginning of his life serving the King of Kings. This was his new commission to proclaim the TRUE Gospel of the Lord Jesus Christ. Eventually the rest of the family saw the changes and within a year they too became born again.

The Oxley family was once again on the move this time to NATO in the Netherlands. It was there that they encountered Americans for the first time. The conviction came also at that time to sever his ties with Freemasonry. After three years working top secret for NATO in Holland he was once again transferred this time to NATO in Norway, where he was led to retire and emigrant to America, eventually becoming along with his wife a proud American citizen. They started a ministry in 1985 and he spoke all over the country and including a trip back to his home land sharing his powerful testimony.

Sadly Mick passed away in his sleep on July 20th 2007. He left a legacy behind of setting the captives free and exposing the evil teachings behind Freemasonry, Islam and Eastern Mysticism.

As Mick's daughter—co-author and manager of *In His Grip Ministry*, is to see this book placed in the hands of those, like my Dad, who seek the truth and want to discover who Jesus really is and commit their lives to Him.

PRAYER OF RELEASE FOR FREEMASONS and Their Descendents

If you were once a Mason or are a descendant of a Mason, we recommend that you pray through the following prayer from your heart. Don't be like the Masons who are given their obligations and oaths one line at a time and without prior knowledge of the requirements. Please read it through first so you know what is involved. It is best to pray this aloud with a Christian witness or counselor present. We suggest a brief pause following each paragraph to allow the Holy Spirit to show any additional issues that may require attention.

"Father God, creator of heaven and earth, I come to you in the name of Jesus Christ your Son, I come as a sinner seeking forgiveness and cleansing from all sins committed against you, and others made in Your image. I honor my earthly father and mother and all my ancestors of flesh and blood, and by the spirit of adoption and godparents, but I utterly turn away from and renounce all their sins on my children and me. I confess and renounce all of my own sins. I renounce and rebuke Satan and every spiritual power of his affecting my family and me.

I renounce and forsake all involvement in Freemasonry or any other lodge or craft by my ancestors and myself. I renounce witchcraft, the principal spirit behind Freemasonry, and I renounce

Baphomet, the Spirit of Antichrist and the curse of the Luciferian doctrine.

I renounce the idolatry, blasphemy I renounce the idolatry, blasphemy, secrecy and deception of Masonry at every level. I specifically renounce the insecurity, the love of position and power, the love of money, avarice or greed, and the pride which would have led my ancestors into Masonry. I renounce all the fears, which held them in Masonry, especially the fears of death, fears of men, and fears of trusting, in the name of Jesus Christ.

I renounce every position held in the lodge by any of my ancestors, including "Tyler", "Master", "Worshipful Master" or any other. I renounce the calling of any man "Master" for Jesus Christ is my only master and Lord, and He forbids anyone else having that title. I renounce the entrapping of others into Masonry, and observing the helplessness of others during the rituals. I renounce the effects of Masonry passed on to me through any female ancestor who felt distrusted and rejected by her husband as he entered and attended any lodge and refused to tell her of his secret activities.

I choose to forgive my family and ancestors for involving themselves for whatever reason in Freemasonry and other occultic practices. The Bible says that unless I forgive, then I will not be forgiven. I also forgive my family for allowing a curse to enter our family tree and causing sickness and disease to come to us.

1st Degree

I renounce the oaths taken and the curses involved in the First or Entered Apprentice degree, especially their effects on the throat and tongue. I renounce the Hoodwink, the blindfold, and its effects on emotions and eyes, including all confusion, fear of the dark, fear of the light, and fear of sudden noises. I renounce the secret word BOAZ, and all that it means. I renounce the mixing and mingling of truth and error, and the blasphemy of this degree of Masonry. I renounce the noose around the neck, the fear of choking and also every spirit causing asthma, hay fever, emphysema and other breathing difficulties. I renounce the compass point, sword of spear held against the breast, the fear of death by stabbing pain, and the fear of heart attack from this degree. In the name of Jesus Christ I now pray for healing of ...(throat, vocal cords, nasal passages, sinus, bronchial tubes etc) for healing of the speech area, and the release of the Word of God to me and through me and my family.

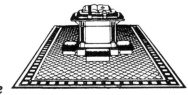

2nd Degree

I renounce the oaths taken and the curses involved in the second or FELLOW CRAFT DEGREE of Masonry, especially the curses on the heart and chest. I renounce the secret words JACHIN and

SHIBBOLETH and all that these mean. I cut off emotional hardness, apathy, indifference, unbelief, and deep anger from my family and me. In the name of Jesus Christ I pray for the healing of.........(the chest/lung /heart area) and also for the healing of my emotions and ask to be made sensitive to the Holy Spirit of God.

3rd Degree

I renounce the oaths taken and the curses involved in the third or Master Mason degree, especially the curses on the stomach and womb area. I renounce the secret words MAHA BONE, MACHABEN, MACHBINNA and TUBAL CAIN, and all that they mean. I renounce the spirit of death from the blows to the head enacted as RITUAL MURDER, the fear of death, false martyrdom, and fear of violent gang attack, assault or rape, and the helplessness of this degree.

I renounce the falling into the coffin or stretcher involved in the ritual of murder. I renounce the false resurrection of this degree, because only Jesus Christ is the Resurrection and the Life!

I also renounce the blasphemous kissing of the Bible on a Witchcraft oath. I cut off all spirits of death, witchcraft and deception and in the name of Jesus Christ I pray for the healing of (The stomach, gall bladder, womb, liver and any other organs of my body affected by Masonry), and I ask for a release of compassion and understanding for my family and me.

Holy Royal Arch Degree

I renounce and forsake the oaths taken and the curses involved in the Holy Royal Arch Degree of Masonry. Especially the oath regarding the removal of the head from the body and the exposing of the brains to the hot sun. I renounce the Mark Lodge, and the mark in the form of squares and angles which marks the person for life. I also reject the jewel or talisman, which may have been made from the mark sign and worn at lodge meetings.

I renounce the false secret name of God JAHBULON, and the password AMMI RUHAMAH and all that they mean. I renounce the false communion or Eucharist taken in this degree, and all the mockery, skepticism and unbelief about the redemptive work of Jesus Christ on the cross of Calvary. I cut off all these curses and their effects on me and my family in the name of Jesus Christ, and I pray for ...(healing of the brain, the mind etc.)

18th Degree

I renounce the oaths taken and the curses involved in the eighteenth degree of Masonry, the MOST WISE SOVERIGN KNIGHT OF THE PELICANS, and the EAGLE and SOVEREIGN PRINCE OF ROSE CROIX OF HEREDOM. I renounce and reject the Pelican witchcraft spirits, as well as the occultic influence of the Rosicrucian's and the Kabala in this degree. I renounce the claim that the death of Jesus Christ was a "dire calamity", and also the deliberate mockery and twisting of the Christian doctrine of Atonement. I renounce the blasphemy and rejection of the deity of Jesus Christ and the secret words IGNE NATURA RENOVATUR INTEGRA and its burning. I renounce the mockery of the communion taken in this degree, including a biscuit, salt and water wine.

I renounce the oaths taken and the curses and penalties involved in the AMERICAN AND GRAND ORIENT LODGES, including the SECRET MASTER DEGREE, its secret password of ADONAIM and its penalties; of the PERFECT MASTER DEGREE, its secret password of MAH-HAH-BONE, and its penalty of being smitten to the earth with a setting maul;

Of the INTIMATE SECRETARY DEGREE, its secret password of JAHOVAH used blasphemously, and its penalties of having my body dissected, and of having my vital organs cut into pieces and thrown to the beasts of the field;

Of the PROVOST AND JUDGE DEGREE, its secret password of HIRUM-TITO-CIVI-KY, and the penalty of having my nose cut off;

Of the INTENDANT OF THE BUILDING DEGREE, of its secret password AKAR-JAI-JAH, and the penalty of having my eyes put out, my body cut in two and exposing my bowels;

Of the ELECTED KNIGHTS OF THE NINE DEGREE, its secret password NEKAM NAKAH, and its penalty of having my head cut off and stuck on the highest pole in the East;

Of the KNIGHT OF THE EAST AND WEST DEGREE, and its secret password ABADDON, and its penalty of incurring the severe wrath of the Almighty Creator of Heaven and Earth.

Of the COUNCIL OF KADOSH GRAND PONTIFF DEGREE, its secret password EMMANUAL, and its penalties;

Of the GRAND MASTER OF SYMBOLIC LODGES DEGREE, it secret password JEKSON/STOLKIN, and its penalties;

Of the NOACHITE OF PRUSSIAN KNIGHT DEGREE, its secret password PELEG, and its penalties;

Of the KNIGHT OF THE ROYAL AXE DEGREE, its secret password NOAH-BEZALEEI-SODONIAS, and all its penalties;

Of the CHIEF OF THE TABERNACLE DEGREE, its secret password URIEL-JEHOVAH, and its penalty that I agree the earth should open up and engulf me to my neck so I perish;

Of the PRINCE OF THE TABERNACLE DEGREE, its penalty that I should be stoned to death and my body left above ground to rot;

Of the KNIGHT OF THE BRAZEN SERPENT DEGREE, its secret password MOSES-JOHANNES, and its penalty that I have my heart eaten by venomous serpents;

Of the PRINCE OF MERCY DEGREE, its secret password GOMEL, JAHOVAH-JACHIN, and its penalty of condemnation and spite by the entire universe;

Of the ILLUSTRIOUS ELECT OF FIFTEEN DEGREE, with its secret password, ELIGNAM, and it's penalties of having my body opened perpendicularly and horizontally, the entrails exposed to the air for eight hours so that flies may prey on then, and for my head to be cut off and placed on a high pinnacle.

Of the SUBLIME KNIGHTS ELECT OF THE TWELVE DEGREES, it's secret password STOLKIN-ADONI, and it's penalty of having my band cut in twain;

Of THE GRAND MASTER ARCHITECT DEGREE, it's secret password, JEHOVAH, and its penalty of having my body given to the beasts of the forest forever as prey;

Of the GRAND ELECT, PERFECT AND SUBLIME MASON DEGREE, its secret password, and its penalty of having my body cut open and my bowels given to vultures for food;

Of the KNIGHTS OF THE EAST DEGREE, it's secret password, RAPH-O-DOM, and its penalties;

Of the PRINCE OF JERUSALEM DEGREE, it's secret password, TEBET-ADAR, and it's penalty of being stripped naked and having my heart pierced with a poniards;

Of the KNIGHT COMMANDER OF THE TEMPLE DEGREE, its secret password, SOLOMON, and its penalty of receiving the severest wrath of the Almighty God inflicted upon me;

Of the KNIGHT COMMANDER OF THE SUN, OR PRINCE ADEPT DEGREE, it's secret password, STIBIUM, and it's penalties of having my tongue thrust through with a red-hot iron, of my eyes being plucked out, my senses of smelling and hearing being removed, of having my hands cut off and in that condition to be left for voracious animals to devour me, or executed by lightening from heaven;

Of the GRAND SCOTTISH KNIGHT OF SAINT ANDREW DEGREE, it's secret password, NEKAMAH-FURLAC, and its penalties;

30th Degree

I renounce the oaths taken and the curses involved in the thirtieth degree of Masonry, the Grand Knight Kadosh and Knight of the Black and White Eagle. I renounce the password, STIBIUM ALKABAR and all it means.

31st Degree

I renounce the oaths taken and the curses involved in the thirty-first degree of Masonry, the Grand Inspector Inquisitor Commander. I renounce all the gods and goddesses of Egypt, which are honored in this degree, including Anubis with the ram's head, Osiris the Sun god, Isis the sister and wife of Osiris and also the moon goddess. I renounce the Soul of immorality, the Chamber of the dead and the false teaching of reincarnation.

The grip
32nd Degree

I renounce the oaths taken and the curses involved in the thirty-second degree of Masonry, the Sublime Prince of the Royal Secret. I renounce Masonry's false Trinitarian deity ALUM, and all its parts; BRAHMA THE CREATOR, VISHNU THE PRESERVER and SHIVA THE DESTROYER.

I renounce the deity of AHURA-MAZDA, the claimed spirit or source of all light, and the worship of fire, which is an abomination to God, and also the drinking from a human skull in many Rites.

York Rite

Knights Templar

I renounce the oaths taken and the curses involved in the York Rite of Freemasonry, including MARK MASTER, PAST MASTER, MOST EXCELLENT MASTER, ROYAL MASTER, SELECT MASTER, SUPER EXCELLENT MASTER, THE ORDERS OF THE RED CROSS, THE KNIGHTS OF MALTA, and THE KNIGHTS TEMPLAR degrees. I renounce the secret words of JOPPA, KEB RAIOTH, and MAHER-SHALAL-HASH-BAZ. I renounce the vows taken on a human skull, the crossed swords, and the curse and death wish of Judas; of having the head cut off and placed on top of a church spire. I renounce the unholy communion and especially of drinking from a human skull in many Rites.

Shriners

(America only—does not apply world-wide)

I renounce the oaths taken and the curses and penalties involved in the ANCIENT ARABIC ORDER OF THE NOBLES OF THE MYSTIC SHRINE.

I renounce the piercing of the eyeballs with a three-edged blade, the flaying of the feet, the madness and the worship of the false god Allah as the god of our fathers. I renounce the hoodwink, the mock hanging, the mock beheading, the mock drinking of the blood of the victim, the mock dog urinating on the initiate, and the offering of urine as a commemoration.

33rd Degree

I renounce the oaths taken and the curses involved in the thirty-third degree of Masonry, the GRAND SOVERIAGN INSPECTOR GENERAL.. I renounce and forsake the declaration that Lucifer is God. I renounce the cable-tow around the neck. I renounce the death wish that the wine drunk from human skull should turn to poison and the skeleton whose cold arms are invited if the oath of this degree is violated. I renounce the three infamous assassins of their grandmaster, law, property and religion, and the greed and witchcraft involved in the attempt to manipulate and control the rest of mankind.

All other degrees

I renounce all the other oaths taken, the rituals of every other degree and the curses involved. I renounce all other lodges and secret societies such as PRINCE HALL FREEMASONRY, MORMONISM, THE ORDER OF AMARANTH, ODDFELLOWSM BUFFALOS, DRUIDS, FORESTERS, ORANGE,

ELKS, MOOSE, AND EAGLES LODGES, THE KU KLUX KLAN, THE GRANGE, THE WOODMEN OF THE WORLD, RIDERS OF THE RED ROBE, THE KNIGHTS OF PYTHIAS, THE MYSTIC ORDER OF THE VEILED PROPHETS OF THE ENCHANTED REALM, THE WOMEN'S ORDERS OF EASTERN STAR, and of the WHITE SHRINE OF JERUSALEM, the girls' order of the DAUGHTERS OF THE EASTERN STAR, THE INTERNATIONAL ORDERS OF JOB'S DAUGHTERS, and of THE RAINBOW, and boys' ORDER OF DE MOLAY, the effects on me and all my family.

I renounce the ancient pagan teaching and symbolism of the First Tracing Board, the Second Tracing Board, and the Third Tracing Board used in the ritual of the Blue Lodge. I renounce the pagan ritual of the "Point within a Circle" with all its bondages and phallus worship. I renounce the occultic mysticism of the black and white mosaic chequered floor with the tessellated boarder and five-pointed blazing star. I renounce the symbol "G" and its veiled pagan symbolism and bondages. I renounce and utterly forsake the Great Architect of The Universe, who is revealed in the higher degrees as Lucifer, and his false claim to be the universal fatherhood of God.

I also renounce the false claim that Lucifer is the Morning Star and Shining One and I declare that Jesus Christ is the Bright and Morning Star of Revelation 22:16.

I renounce the All-Seeing Third Eye of Freemasonry or Horus in the forehead and its pagan and occult symbolism. I renounce all false communions taken, all mockery of the redemptive work of Jesus Christ on the cross of Calvary, all unbelief, confusion and depression, and all worship of Lucifer as God. I renounce and forsake the lie of Freemasonry that man is not sinful, but merely imperfect, and so can redeem him through good works. I rejoice that the Bible states that I cannot do a single thing to earn my salvation, but that I can only be saved by grace through faith in Jesus Christ and what He accomplished on the Cross of Calvary.

I renounce all fear of insanity, anguish, death wishes, suicide and death in the name of Jesus Christ. Jesus Christ conquered death, and He alone holds the keys of death and hell, and I rejoice that He holds my life in His hands now. He came to give me life abundantly and eternally, and I believe His promises.

I renounce all anger, hatred, murderous thoughts, revenge, retaliation, spiritual apathy, false religion, all unbelief, especially unbelief in the Holy Bible as God's Word, and all compromise of God's Word. I renounce all spiritual searching into false religions, and all striving to please God. I rest in the knowledge that I have found my Lord and Savior Jesus Christ, and that He has found me.

A Masonic apron

I will burn all objects in my possession which connect me with all lodges and occultic organizations, including Masonry, Witchcraft, and Mormonism, and all regalia, aprons, books of rituals, rings and other jewellery.

I renounce the effects these or other objects of Masonry, such as the compass, the square, the noose or the blindfold have had on me or my family, in Jesus name.

(All participants should now be invited to sincerely carry out the following)

1. Symbolically remove the blindfold (hoodwink) and give it to the Lord for disposal;

2. In the same way, symbolically remove the veil of mourning;

3. Symbolically cut and remove the noose from around the neck, gather it up with the cable-tow running down the body and give it all to the Lord for His disposal;

4. Renounce the false Freemasonry marriage covenant, removing from the 4th finger of the right hand the ring of this false marriage covenant, giving it to the Lord to dispose it;

5. Symbolically remove all Freemasonry regalia and Armor, especially the Apron.

6. Symbolically remove the chains and bondages of Freemasonry from your body.

7. Invite Participants to repent of and seek forgiveness for having walked on all unholy ground, including Freemasonry Lodges and temples, including any Mormon or other occultic/Masonic organizations

8. Symbolically remove the ball and chain from the ankles.

Proclaim that Satan and his demons no longer have any legal rights to mislead and manipulate the person/s seeking help.

Holy Spirit, I ask that you show me anything else, which I need to do or to pray so that my family and I may be totally free from the consequences of the sins of Masonry, Witchcraft, Mormonism and Paganism.

(Pause, while listening to God, and pray as the Holy Spirit leads you.)

Now dear Father God, I ask humbly for the blood of Jesus Christ, Your Son, to cleanse me from all these sins I have confessed and renounced, to cleanse my spirit, my soul, my mind, my emotions and every part of my body which has been affected by these sins, in Jesus' name!

I renounce every evil spirit associated with Masonry and Witchcraft and all other sins, and I command in the name of Jesus Christ for Satan and every evil spirit to be bound and to leave me now, touching or harming no-one, and go to the place appointed for you by the Lord Jesus, never to return to me or my family. I call on the name of the Lord Jesus to be delivered of these spirits, in accordance with the many promises of the Bible. I ask to be delivered of every spirit of sickness, infirmity, curse, affliction addiction, disease or allergy associated with these sins I have confessed and renounced.

I surrender to God's Holy Spirit and to no other spirit all the places in my life where these sins have been. I ask you, Lord, to baptize me in Your Holy Spirit now according to the promises in Your Word. I take to myself the whole Armor of God in accordance with Ephesians 6, and rejoice in its protection as Jesus surrounds me and fills me with His Holy Spirit. I enthrone you Lord Jesus; in my heart for You are my Lord and my Savior the source of eternal life. Thank you Father God for your mercy, forgiveness and Your love, In the name of Jesus Christ, Amen."

With the exception of using Americanized spelling and on page 1 the paragraph on forgiveness, this prayer is taken from "Unmasking Freemasonry" —Removing the Hoodwink" by Selwyn Stevens, (ISBN 0 9583417-3-7) published by Jubilee Publishers, PO box 36-044, Wellington 6330, New Zealand. Copying of this prayer is both permitted and encouraged provided reference is made to where it comes from. Written testimonies of changed lives and healings are welcome.

If additional prayer and ministry are required following the above prayer, please contact one of those listed below. For reasons of distance, they may refer you to someone closer to you.

Ministry Help and Contact Information

Out of USA

Selwyn Stevens Jubilee Essential Resources. Po Box 36-044, Wellington 6330, New Zealand
Phone (644) 564-7688

Ellel Ministries RR#1 Orangeville, Ontario L9W 2Y8 Canada
Phone (519) 941-0929

USA

IN HIS GRIP MINISTRIES 206 Paradise Shores Rd Crescent City, Florida 32112
Phone (386) 698-2553

Gene Moody DELIVERANCE MINISTRY 14930 Jefferson Highway, Baton Rouge LA 70817
Phone (225)755-8870

David & Donna Carrico 5220 Ashley Drive, Evansville, Indiana 47711
Phone (812) 477-6338

Recommended Reading

"Prayer of Release"....................Selwyn Stevens

"Removing the Hoodwink".........Selwyn Stevens

"The Dark Side of Freemasonry".....Ed Decker

All of the above material and many more may be purchased from "In His Grip Ministries, Inc."

Works Cited

- Hannah, Waltar. Darkness Visible. Augustine Press: London, England. 1952.

- Newton, Joseph Fort, Litt.D. The Builders. Macoy Publishing and Masonic Supply Company: Richmond, Virginia. 1951.

- Short, Martin. Inside the Brotherhood. Dorset Press: New York. 1989.

Please contact us if this book made an impact in your life. We want to rejoice with you!

email: ingrip@msn.com

Made in the USA
Charleston, SC
17 February 2013